Poems From The Heart

RENEE G. STEWART

Order this book online at www.trafford.com/07-0386
or email orders@trafford.com

Most Trafford titles are also available at major online book retailers.

Note for Librarians: A cataloguing record for this book is available from Library and Archives Canada at www.collectionscanada.ca/amicus/index-e.html

ISBN: 978-1-4251-1981-2

We at Trafford believe that it is the responsibility of us all, as both individuals and corporations, to make choices that are environmentally and socially sound. You, in turn, are supporting this responsible conduct each time you purchase a Trafford book, or make use of our publishing services. To find out how you are helping, please visit www.trafford.com/responsiblepublishing.html

Our mission is to efficiently provide the world's finest, most comprehensive book publishing service, enabling every author to experience success. To find out how to publish your book, your way, and have it available worldwide, visit us online at www.trafford.com/10510

www.trafford.com

North America & international
toll-free: 1 888 232 4444 (USA & Canada)
phone: 250 383 6864 • fax: 250 383 6804 • email: info@trafford.com

The United Kingdom & Europe
phone: +44 (0)1865 487 395 • local rate: 0845 230 9601
facsimile: +44 (0)1865 481 507 • email: info.uk@trafford.com

10 9 8 7 6 5 4

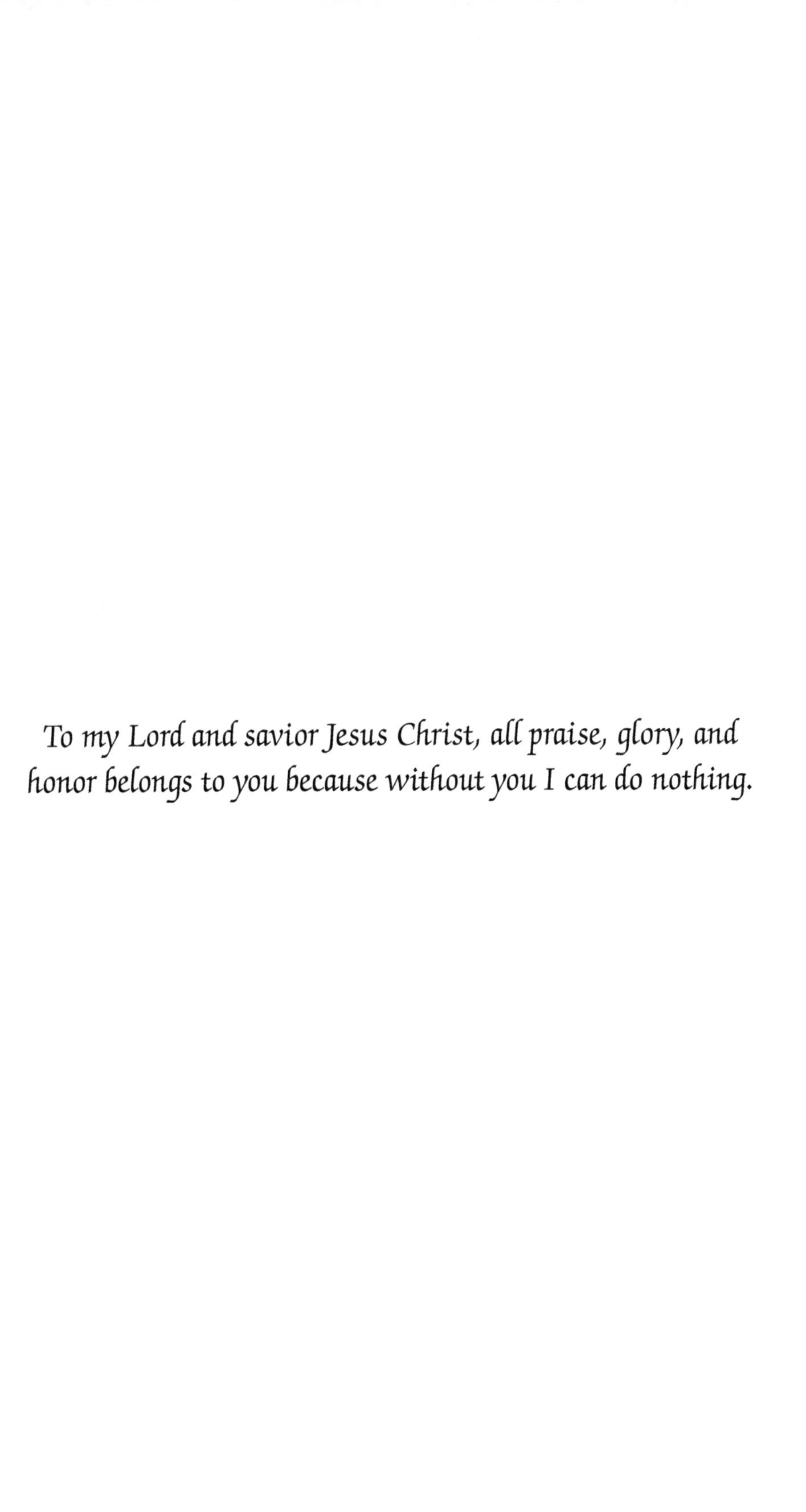

To my Lord and savior Jesus Christ, all praise, glory, and honor belongs to you because without you I can do nothing.

ACKNOWLEDGMENTS

With Special Thanks To:

To Walter, thank you for believing in the gifts that God has bestowed upon me.

To my three miracles, Elijah, Ahmad and Nhylah, thank you all for being such wonderful children and thank you for all the hard work on the photos in this book. Ahmad, the cover design is wonderful!

To my wonderful mother who has given me life, I appreciate you more and more each day, thank you for loving me unconditionally.

To my dad, Roland Elliott thanks for being there whenever I call.

To my spiritual teachers, Pastor Alma Horne, Evangelist Gladys McNeil, Mother Ozella Hammrick, Prophetess Monica Langley, Pastor Moses L. Scott and 1st Lady Regina Scott, thank you all so much for your continued prayers and for being the greater cloud of witnesses in my life. Your determination to rightly divide the word of God spoke life to my soul, thank you for crying loud and sparing not and most of all for keeping it real!

To my close friends, Pamela, Carolyn (Moose), and Demetria thank you all for your prayers and encouragement. Thank you all for being there when I needed you most.

To my best friend Loretta, I am glad that God allowed you to enter into my life, he knew just what I needed, when I needed it. I am grateful for you never changing and always PRAYING!

To my family and friends, I love you all.

Table of Contents

Devotion and Encouragement

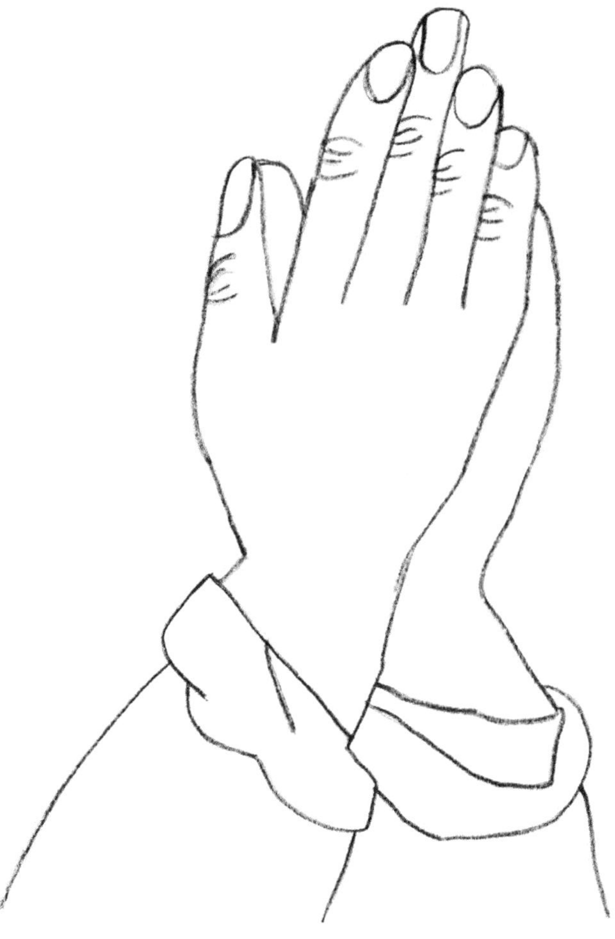

Trust In the Lord

When troubles seem hard to bare and you can't see your way through
Remember deep down inside your heart the Lord is right beside you
When times come in your life and your heart is filled with pain
Just fall down on your knees and call on Jesus name
When it seems like all hope is gone and you don't know what to do
Wait on the lord; he'll work things out for you
When situations happen around you and you just don't understand
Don't try to figure it out, place it in the master's hands

"Continue to trust in the Lord"

Be Grateful

Lord help me not to take for granted the life you've given to me
Help me to appreciate the fact that salvation is free
Teach me how to love my neighbor as you have commanded me
And help me to always remember, I am nothing without thee!
Help me to be grateful for the simple things in life
Help me to keep my heart pure, free from envy and strife
Teach me Lord, how to forgive and how to forget
Help me to treat everyone with much deserved respect
Help me to always remember the storms you've brought me through
Realizing that I could not have made it, had it not been for you.

Oh Lord

Lord, why have thou forsaken me?
Why have thou not set my soul free?

I cried out and prayed to you but you have not helped me yet
Is it because I'm still a sinner, and I'm not at my best?

Lord please help me, I can't make it on my own
I trust that you will soon be here if I keep holding on

Lord I prayed and pleaded with you
And now I've become so desperate that I don't know what to do!

I don't know how but I hope I find peace soon
So that this burden in my heart can quickly be removed

God Is In Control

Trials and tribulations they say come to make us strong
Although I don't always feel this way when everything seems to be going wrong

I try to stay encouraged and hold my head up high
Yet within the midnight hour all I can do is cry

Trying hard to understand just why I'm going through
Not getting any answers or knowing exactly what to do

Praying everyday for the Lord to show me a way out
Fighting the devil daily as he tries to fill my mind with doubt

Realizing that there's really nothing else I can do
Just stand still, believe that God knows just how to bring me through

Not always understanding but trying to trust and believe
God takes care of the birds and I know he will take care of me

I've come too far to turn my back on what I believe in my soul
No matter what situation I find myself in, I know that God is always in control

My Midnight

As I sit in my midnight no light can be seen
Searching deeply within myself trying to understand what it all means
Longing for daylight to somehow break through
Only to long in vain, watching the midnight dew
Falling constantly time after time,
Not even a twinkle of light ahead can I find
When will I see the breaking of day?
When will my midnight fade away?
Crying many tears while I sit and wait
Searching for a peace of mind, waiting for daybreak
Keeping the faith and believing that one day I'll see
A day filled with sunshine, light, and peace
Holding on in my midnight and praying one day I'll find
A life filled with joy, and everyday filled with sunshine

Someone Cares

When situations arise and you don't seem to understand
When you feel as though you have done just about all that you can
Someone Cares

When it seems like nothing is turning out right
When it seems like your hurting day and night
Someone Cares

When you feel the need to talk to someone and no one is there,
When troubles get you down and it seems like no one cares
Someone Cares

When all else fails and you have no where to turn
Turn around and look at me because I'm the one who cares

Don't Give Up

Sometimes when troubles come our way we stumble and we fall
But God wants you to know that he's your all and all

Sometimes burdens seem so hard to bare
But God wants you to know he'll always be there

When it seems like your carrying the weight of the world on your shoulders
God wants you to know that soon it will all be over

When no one else seem to understand
God wants you to know that he'll lend you a helping hand

When all else fails and you feel stuck
God is saying my child hold on, please don't give up!

You're Never Alone

When life's trials begin to get you down
When friends and loved ones are no where to be found

In the late night hour fear fills your mind
You lay awake, peace you try hard to find

Sometimes worrying if the pain will go away
Sometimes not knowing if you'll see another day,

Just remember the words that Jesus said
Let not your heart be troubled neither let it be afraid

No matter what the devil tries to tell you, just keep the faith and remain strong
Always remember as long as you have Jesus, you're never alone

Whose I Am

Sitting here feeling lonely in a room full of people,
Could it be that I'm strange, or that no one here is my equal?

Have I reached a place that no one else can see?
Have I come to realize that there truly is only one me?

Realizing every day that there really is something unique inside
No longer desiring to hang my head and hide

Ready to endure the trials that face me everyday
Knowing that through it all my God will make a way

No longer fearing in my heart that I'm just not good enough
Believing that I can do anything if in God I continue to trust

Burdens get heavy, sometimes they make me bend
But that is when I get on my knees and talk to my friend

See, he doesn't care about the fact that my hair is not done
He doesn't care that my stockings may have a run

He's not concerned about the mistakes I made on yesterday
He only cares about the way I'm living my life today

He knows the very heart of me so there's nothing I can hide
He knows just what I feel, so there is no need to lie

I'm a strong black woman who has overcome many pains!
Yet I'm still standing, holding on in Jesus name

Yes I have some bruises, some scars that may never go away
But they won't control my life because those wounds were yesterday

Yesterday is gone, never to return again
Today is a new day, a new adventure to begin

Whether with friends or on the road by myself,
As long as I have Jesus, I don't need anybody else.
I know whose I am!

Mistakes

Lord, I've made so many mistakes,
Always trying to remember the give and takes,
You let me go so far before you bring me back
You're telling me I should know now for a fact
That I can do nothing without you
And only you can see me through
All of the good and all the bad that I undertake
And that to stray away from you would only be another mistake.

Someone Is Watching Over You!

When troubles and confusion get you down and you don't know what to do,
Always remember that there's someone watching over you

When you feel that you can't make it, and you can't see your way
Remember there is an angel beside you that will never let you stray

When walls are built in front of you and you can't get around
Stop and consider your angel and let him knock it down

When it seems like no one understands and you feel lost
Count on that angel and let him be the boss!

The Dawning of a New Day

Early I rise as I fall on my knees to pray
Asking God to strengthen me as I go along my way

Realizing that he's kept me safely through another night
Watching over me as I slept, holding my soul tight

For the Devil desires to come and steal my soul away
Knowing whose I am, he tries to make me stray

Many hard trials some big and some small
Rejoicing because God delivers me from them all

Clinging desperately as I search for peace of mind
Realizing that the peace I seek, only in Jesus can I find

Thanking the Lord daily keeps my mouth filled with praise
Knowing that tomorrow begins the dawning of a new day!

I Wonder Why?

I've moved 400 miles away with the hope of starting anew
Yet now I find myself wondering if it was the right thing to do

Such a new environment, nothing that reminds me of the old
Yet within my heart I feel like there's nothing to hold

No solid foundation to physically hold on to
Just my faith in God and my prayers to see me through

Sometimes crying in the late hours of the night
Taking medication just to ease the fright

Fear of not knowing what tomorrow will hold for me
Not knowing how or what I will feed my family

So many questions running through my mind
No one has the answer I just pray and ask God Why?

All In God's Hands

Who would have ever imagined that 9/11 would be the day
Someone so cold and heartless would come and take our loved ones away
So many unspoken words, so many things left undone
Yet so many happy memories of days filled with fun
Although we're left with many emotions, anger,
hurt and loneliness just to name a few
There is comfort in knowing we are not alone, other's share in our loss too
Now we must go on, find the strength to move ahead day by day
Allowing God to lead and guide us along the way
Why it all happened we may never understand
But let's find peace in knowing that they're all in God's hands.

Who Can Find A Virtuous Woman?

Who can find a virtuous woman?
There's none fairer in the land
Perfect in the eyes of God
Yet remaining a mystery to man
The beauty she possesses lies far beyond the skin
Each and every trial sparks a greater strength within
Though the storms rage and the winds swiftly blow
The gentleness of her smile remains and no one would ever know
The tears shed in the late night hours; God catches them in one hand
Storing them all up to pour out blessings according to his master plan,
Who can find a virtuous woman, strong, upheld as a tower
Sitting with scars of wars won by God's unfailing power
And those she's carried through the fire on the sacrifices of her soul
Come home to show their homage and to shelter her with love
Who can find this virtuous woman is there one in the land?
Yes, there she sits glowing in the palms of Gods blood stained hands

"Thank you for all the love, caring and sacrifices you've made on my behalf"

W.O.M.A.N

W- Is for the Godly wisdom that we possess
O- Is for the only begotten son who gave his life so we could be blessed
M- Is for the mighty acts he has given us the power to perform
A- Is for the alter in our hearts where the love of God belongs
N- Is for the New Life we seek to obtain

Woman the bridegroom cometh, will you be ready when he comes?

Satan I Know You!

So many trials and so much pain
Why does the devil continually try to make me go insane?
Why do you continue to try and make me doubt?
Why can't you see, I know what you're all about?
All you want to do is kill, steal and destroy
Toss the saints of God around just like some little toy,
But what you fail to understand is that we're more powerful, yes it's true
Every time you think were on your side, we get away from you
See our father loves us and he holds our life in his hands
So no matter how hard you try, he has the master plan
He has already decided that we belong to him
So no matter what you say, we don't have to sin
So go away Satan, just leave us alone
We love our Father and he keeps us strong

His Will

Oh my Lord could this really be
The love of my life being taken away from me
Laying there in that hospital bed starring off into space
I can't help but wonder if he will remember my face
This sickness came on so quickly that I haven't had time to think
I just sit here by your side and watch you as you sleep
Praying the entire night that in the morning you'll still be here
Not wanting to let you go, desiring to keep you near
Sitting here wondering is there an unspoken word that needs to be said
Are there things undone, messages that have gone unread
Suddenly I stop and remember that God knows best
I must hold on to my faith and let my mind rest
Knowing that the Lord knows what's best for me
For it is his will that must be done for all eternity.

Keeping the Faith

Everyday when I awake
I lift my eyes towards heaven
Realizing that I'm still here
I thank God for his blessing.

Not always happy,
Days often filled with pain
Yet being grateful knowing
That there will be sunshine after the rain.

Keeping the faith in spite of my circumstance
I trust and I believe
Holding on to God's promise
To never leave or forsake me.

Knowing this one thing God's word
Will always hold true
God will not put more than you can bare upon you.

Proud To Be Me

I deserve to have the best though everyone may say
But I would have to accept my life either way,
Regardless of whether my dreams ever come true, or whether I ever succeed
I'm proud to be alive and well, and even happier to be able to breathe
Though life is never what we plan it to be
I'm proud of those things I have accomplished and even prouder to be me

I Apologize

I knew you were sick and I didn't stop by
I could give a lot of excuses all beginning with "I"
I was just so busy,
I just simply forgot,
I would have come but I knew to many visitors would be a lot
I got caught up in running all around
I didn't have a ride, and I couldn't get downtown
These are a few of the excuses we as saints often use,
But the righteous thing to do is just to tell the truth
I have no excuses; I was just consumed within myself
Thinking only of me and mine, and forgetting about your health
Breaking Gods commandments to love one another
Not stopping to remember that you are my brother
Realizing that words could never undo the wrongs that have been done unto you,
Please let me just start by saying, I truly apologize to you

Christ Led

March 19th, the day it all begun
God blessed my life with the miracle of Elijah, my first born son
He was small yet long and a bit funny looking to me
So amazed that he was born I would sit and watch him sleep
As he lay there smiling watching the angels as they played
I sit there envisioning him going off to first grade
Eyes all aglow as he smiles at the sound of my voice
Wanting to put him down only he feels that's a bad choice
As he grows and begins to get a mind of his own
My heart begins to get heavy realizing he's only a loan
God has given him to me but only for a season
He must fulfill Gods purpose for his life, God must have a reason
Seeing how the devil desired many times to take his life.
But God in his power stepped in and made the devil think twice
He is God's chosen vessel and I know there are challenges ahead
But the battle is already won as long as he's Christ led!

Friendship

A Friendship Earned

One day we were talking, the next day we were sharing tears
Soon we began to tell each other secrets and disclose our fears

Not knowing that with every minute the love was beginning to grow
Trying desperately to hold emotions inside, not wanting to let them show

What started out as a simple friendship has flourished into love
No one will ever understand but me, you, and the Lord up above

Yes we fall out and we often times disagree
But I know in my heart that I love you and you love me

No matter what the changes, I'll always be there for you
Holding you up when you're falling down, helping you to go through

You mean more to me than words or gifts can ever express
My greatest concern, is for your happiness

So don't ever think that my love comes along with conditions
Know that it is genuine and definitely without restrictions

Even if it means that I have to turn and walk away
Then I do it with a broken heart and a smile on my face

Knowing that true happiness is what I've given you
Joy in the unhappy times along with a laugh or two

So I want to let you know that no matter which way this road may turn
Our friendship is a reward that the both of us have earned

The Sorrows of Friendship

The pains of friendship have bruised my heart
Time has gone by so quickly, I don't know where to start
We had a disagreement as friends sometimes do
But should that end the friendship that we both hold so true?
True friendship last through many ups and downs
Sometimes as we go through, we may wear a slight frown
Knowing in our hearts that things will soon be better
Waiting for that time when we will be back together
We are both children of God and some things just shouldn't be
If we don't agree, we should be able to come together in unity
Not allowing the enemy to take full control
Not allowing the anger to build and vex our soul
I take this time to say that I am Godly sorry for the pain I have caused you
Just know that in my heart our friendship will forever remain true
If you choose not to remain friends, then I will understand
Just know that I am here if you ever need a helping hand

What Is A Friend?

A friend is someone to talk to when I'm feeling down
A friend is someone I feel close to even when their not around
A friend is someone who loves you no matter what you do
A friend is someone who loves you just because your you
A friend is someone who holds you and makes everything alright
A friend is someone you can call on any time of night
A friend is someone who will forgive even your biggest mistakes
A friend is there to share everything even your heartaches
A friend is there through thick and thin
and if you fall down they will help you up again
I'm glad you're my friend

Friendship Reply

The words you express so heartfelt and warm
Helping me to stand and continue to hold on

Realizing that you're not able to take the pain away
Able to smile just knowing you're willing to go with me all the way

Lending a listening ear when I get overwhelmed
Even a shoulder to cry on, space when I need to scream and yell

So here's my hand just hold on to it tight
Help me to continue on, strengthen me for the fight

I'm glad I'm not alone, even happier to know you care
Praying and loving me through it all, encouraging me to hang in there

Girlfriends

"CRAZY" you see that's our middle names
Hanging out, shopping around, or just playing games

Nothing is out of the ordinary when it comes to me and you
We laugh together and yes we cry together too

I make you angry, and you make me mad
Then after a few days were back together and in our hearts were glad

Glad to be smiling again, no longer biting off heads
Instead were smiling so hard were both turning a shade red

Everyone thinks were nuts the way we make each other act
The way we can just look at each other and both begin to laugh

I call it a friendship, that's very rare these days
Not many come to know it, and others just let it slip away

But I'm glad that every day with you a new adventure begins
And within my heart and mind we will forever be girlfriends

Always There

You were there when I was hurting, sad and full of fear
You were there waiting with outstretched arms, wiping away every tear

You were there when I would fall and make a mistake
You were there sometimes angry, sometimes with looks of heartache

You were there when I was happy, filled with unspeakable joy
You were there when I felt like giving up, didn't think I could take anymore

You were there to hold my hand and strengthen me through prayer
You were there even when you were tired, still lending a listening ear

You were there to laugh with me and share my secrets too
You were there even when I wouldn't talk asking "little-one what did you do"?

You were there when I felt lonely; felt like no one could understand my pain
You were there telling me to trust God, read his word,
especially when troubles flow like rain

You were there when I was sick always by my bedside
You were there and cared so much that you were willing to fight

You have been by my side through thick and thin showing how much you care,
You see, from the time we've met you have always been there

Thank you for being my best friend

The Only Way to Have a Friend

The only way to have a friend is to be one yourself
The only way to keep a friend is to sometimes give from our wealth

For friendship must be double fold, each one must do their part
Feelings true and real that come from the heart

If you would say, they are my friend then no on else will do
But you must say, I am their friend and prove that fact to be true!

What is a Sister?

A sister is there for you when you're feeling down
A sister is one who you feel close to even when their not around
A sister is the one you can be yourself with, without feeling ashamed
A sister is the one who knows you, not just by your name
A sister is the one you call on late at night
A sister is there for you when your wrong and when your right
A sister is one you can lean on when things are going wrong
A sister is there for you when you feel your strength is gone
A sister will not walk on you when you're feeling low
A sister would know when you're hurting, even if you don't let it show
A sister is there for you even when you make a mistake
A sister would even share in your heartache
Although they grow up and sometimes go separate ways
Real sisters can always remember the good old days
Somehow both sisters never seem to reach the top at the same time
But the one on the top will always reach down and help the other to climb
Sisters remain connected from the depths of their heart
No matter what the differences are, true sisters never part

I'm Always Here for You

If ever you feel lonely, like no one understands
Remember I'm here waiting with open outstretched hands

Whenever your pathway gets cloudy and life seems unfair
Remember my dear child, I am always there

Whenever you feel like crying to let off a little steam
Remember my shoulder is here, all you have to do is lean

Whenever you're not strong, I will be your friend
I'll pick you up and carry you until the very end

I Look

As I look I can see, the wonder in your eyes
As I look I can see, the secrets you try to hide

As I look I can see, those true feelings you try not to let show
As I look I can see, you praying that no one will ever know

As I look I can see, the tear tracks on your cheek
As I look I can see the hurt that you feel now is deep

As I look I can see the turmoil and strife
As I look I can see you struggle as you fight

As I look I can see, sometimes you feel like no one will understand
As I look I can see your feeling as if there's no one to hold your hand

As I look I can't help but wonder why I see you so clear
As I look I can't help but wonder why God placed me here

Here, where I can see the hurt you are going through
Here where I can feel the pain the way you do

As I look I can't help but wonder why you don't seem to understand
As I look I can't help but wonder why you won't let me hold your hand

As your going through this storm know that I am here
Not to sit in judgment but to express how much I care

How deeply I am moved when the tears fall from your eyes
How I can feel the weight you carry when upon your breast I lye

How I would if I could, take all the pain away
Just to hear your laughter or see that smile on your face

I am here for the listening, hugging, or whatever you may need
Just open up your heart, look at me and you will see
Just how true a friend I can be

A Blessing to Me

There whenever I needed you, always lending a helping hand
Never asking any questions just offering to do what you can
Not many people possess a genuine gift of agape love
This ingrown gift is given from God up above
God has blessed me to have friends as special as you
To turn to when I need a hand to help me make it through
Some people you meet you sometimes try hard to forget
Then there are others you meet and they bless your life the best

You've Blessed My Life

All that you've done, words could never express
The way you've touched my life I can say that I'm truly blessed

There by my side when I felt like all hope was gone
Praying for me and encouraging me to hold on

Wanting so often to give up and fight no more
Yet you were there telling me that this battle I must endure

Crying many days and pacing the floors at night
Finding comfort in knowing you were on my side

Going through many trials while you held my hand
Opening my eyes after surgery and to my surprise, there you stand

Sometimes going through misunderstandings and refusing to speak
But knowing within our hearts the enemy we would defeat

Many spoken words some not so nice but true
We worked so well together simply because you were real with me, and I with you

I have to go away; I must now take my leave
But I go with tears of joy knowing that you remain a part of me

You hold a place in my heart that time will never erase
Because we share a special bond and we've shared a special place

A friendship that not many ever come to know
One that makes me feel close to you no matter how far away I go

I'll miss seeing you but I know you're by my side
Be happy in knowing that you have not only saved, but you've also blessed my life

Sincerity

We've shared a lot and we became close friends
We've ended the friendship several times only to become friends again

There was so much sincere love between us that it became frightening to me
Although we made a few mistakes we knew some things we had to let be

There were so many emotions, so many unspoken words
Some words spoken in anger and causing a lot of hurt

I tried to be sincere and prove my friendship was true
I'm sorry I couldn't be all you wanted me to

Neither of us planned for things to turn out this way
and we can't erase what's already been done
I believe that everything happens for a reason; you
learn from the mistakes and try to move on

God doesn't condone any of our wrongs
He allows us a free will to decide things on our own

I carry a lot of guilt deep down within my heart
I've prayed and asked God to allow me a brand new start

I'm praying that the Lord will purify my thoughts and my mind
I'm praying that one day you will forgive me and realize
that my feelings were never lies

We were best friends or at least we were in my eyes
But you opened my eyes with the tears you've cause me to cry

I believed that you cared and I soon discovered I was mistaken
It was just my own twisted imagination

But now I know the truth and I must continue to move on
I can't drown in my sorrows, I must remain strong

I want to apologize for all the hurt and pain I put you through
I pray that you believe me when I say, I never meant to hurt you

It breaks my heart just knowing the pain I've caused you
while trying to find real love and inner peace
I ask that you will someday find it in your heart to sincerely forgive me

Far Beyond the Sky

As the sun sets and the dawn of a new day begins
I can't help but think about you, my dear friend
I imagine you sitting there with swollen tear filled eyes
Wondering how you can escape the pain, where can you run and hide
There is a place you know, where you can lay your burdens down
A place where all your bad situations will be turned around
I know sometimes it feels as though you could just loose your mind
Don't worry, hold on, help is coming and it will be there in the nick of time
Cry if you must, scream, and yell out the pain!
Just don't forget to keep calling on Jesus name
He is your peace in the midst of the storm
And he has promised never to leave you alone
So as you journey through this midnight, hold your head up and say
I know through it all I will see the breaking of a new day
Pick yourself up, wipe your weeping eyes
Look towards the hills from whence cometh your
help, it comes from far beyond the sky

Who You Are

Someone who listens with the passion of your heart
Someone who's willing to stand by your side to help you make a new start

Someone who listens to what's coming from inside
Not sitting in judgment or just going along for the ride

The one who puts a smile on your face when you want to breakdown and cry
The one who prays you through when deep inside you no longer want to fight

The one who assures you that everything will turn out fine
The one who sees through the rainy days and shows you the sunshine

No words could begin to explain the "YOU" that I see
No words could ever express who you are to me

"Thank you for being my friend"

Do You Know

True friendship is something that comes from the heart
It's not some emotion that stops and then restarts
True friendship is a bond that's created from within
No one has to tell you, your heart will know a true friend
A true friend will be there when everyone else is gone
Crying with you and praying, helping you to be strong
True friends are never envious no matter what the circumstance
They will be there encouraging you to view your life with a second glance
True friendships are rare and not many come to know its joys
God knows just what you need and he'll send a true friend, not a decoy
Some associations are only in your life for a season
But when a true friend comes along they are there
for life and they don't need a reason
True friendship takes residence deep within the heart
No matter how the challenges come true friendships never part

The Characteristics of You

The contents of this box exemplifies who you are to me
The soft spoken words that put a weary heart at ease
The thoughtful ways you show by always giving of yourself
Never ever hesitating to give of your wealth
You are truly an example of what a child of God should possess
Love, Patience, Understanding, Longsuffering and genuine Kindness

Night Vision

Silent night softly creeping in my head
Wondering day by day why I'm so afraid
No one to talk to, only visions in my mind
Tears streaming down my face as peace I try to find
Peace that passes all understanding and gives pure clarity
Releasing the turmoil from within setting my soul free
Complete freedom, does one ever come to know?
Freedom defines love, and not many ever come to show
Days filled with confusion with only one mission ahead
Counting down the hours when my mind will again be filled with dread
That dreaded night vision, eyes flooded with tears
Sleepless nights haunting me, tossing, turning in my fears

Love and Marriage

Farewell My Friend

A year has gone by and nothing has changed
You still insist on playing the same old game

You said that it was over; you no longer had feelings in your heart
Yet as I watch you near her I see your feelings for her never did depart

The passion in your eyes for her is the passion that I once called my own
Now I cringe with your every touch wondering if we're ever really all alone

Am I the one you see when you close your eyes?
Is it me you're truly yearning in the midst of your sighs?

I refuse to compete with an infatuation that you refuse to admit exists
Yet every touch and every look reminds me of the day you two kissed

I've prayed so long for the Lord to free me from this pain
Now I'm beginning to feel like my prayers are all in vain

Some things we desire we know are out of the will of Christ
But it's truly up to us to decide if were going to do what's right

You've hurt me in the past and I refuse to be hurt again
Farewell my husband, my lover, my friend

Every Beat of My Heart

With every beat of my heart I can feel the pain
The longer you are away from me the more I feel I'm going in sane

When you touch me I feel like I'm alive
When we make love, I feel as though I can take wings and fly

But yet it's all a dream from which I don't want to awake
Knowing that when I open my eyes my heart will begin to break

Awaiting that final moment when you're back in my arms
Holding and caressing me, sheltering me from harm

To once again look into your sparkling eyes
To have you laying gently, between my thighs

If loving you is wrong I don't want to be right
I know who's in my heart both day and night

When the phone rings I jump up to answer it with glee
Knowing your loving voice is on the other end waiting to excite me

Whatever it takes I'll do to keep our love alive
Every hour, minute, and second, on this I will thrive

So let's just say that our end will always be our start
And I will continue to love you with every beat of my heart.

You'll always belong To Me

Whenever I feel lonely I find security in your embrace
Knowing you are a product of God's amazing grace

I'm so blessed to have you in my life
Sometimes I lay awake just remembering that special night

When we share our differences the ecstasy goes untold
Only the moment of exhaustion shows how our love unfolds

You've given me more pleasure than any I've known before
Yet you belong to another, this fact I'm forced to endure

In my heart I long to be your one and only
Realizing that I too have my own responsibility

When all around me seems to be going wrong
I know that I can find comfort wrapped in your arms

Often times I am afraid that our love is not enough
Sometimes I get confused when our situation gets real rough

But I know what I feel inside is true
You love me and yes I love you too

I don't know where or when our roads will take a turn
All I know is here and now, and the touch that I yearn

You are the object of my desire, my soul mate you see
And no matter what the outcome, in my heart you'll always belong to me.

Real Love

R - Is for the right words spoken at the right time
E - Is for the everlasting emotions that flow from your heart to mine
A - Is for the alluring look in your eyes every time we meet
L - Is for the longevity you show when you're making love to me

L - Is for the love we share that none other will ever know
O - Is for the orgy form of fun we always let show
V - Is for the variety of positions we express
E - Is for our everlasting happiness

Put it all together and "REAL LOVE" is what you'll find
One that will surely last until the end of time

SOMEDAY, SOMEWAY

How do you let go without crying?
How do you say good-bye without feeling like part of you is dying?
Sleepless nights trying to figure it all out
Trying to believe with my heart, and erase all the doubt
Trying hard to understand what's making this all so hard
Realizing that the pain I feel can't be put into words like a card
Not understanding why the pain in my heart won't subside
No matter how hard my feelings, I fight to hide
Trying to prove to you that I can stand on my own
But realizing all the while that I can't endure this feeling of being alone
Can't stand not having someone to call my own
Can't stand you ignoring me and wanting to be left alone
Not trying to hurt you in any way
You know I'm going to love you forever and a day
Don't know what it is that makes me so insecure of your love for me
Maybe it's because I've been hurt so much that I'm afraid to love freely
Can't explain why I don't want to share,
Can't explain why I hate feeling that she was there
All I can say is I love you and I hate what I've become
But it doesn't really help me because the damage to my heart has already been done
You have a hold on my heart deep down where no one else can see
So what am I to do now, what happens to me?
Not meaning to sound mean or to sound like a little child
I just don't like the feelings I get whenever she's around
I don't like loving on condition and neither do you
But it seems like we can only be together as long
as she can remain in your heart too
Occupying a place that obviously my love can't reach
I guess my loving you was not enough, although I thought it would be
I know what you tell me and how you say you love me so,
But in order to free you I'll back up and somehow let go
I don't want to cause you any sadness or pain
I just can't survive the pain in my heart, knowing she is there over and over again
I love you but you need to choose,
I love you but, I must find a way to turn loose.

MY HEART BELONGS TO YOU

From the moment I saw you I felt my heart skip a beat
Trying desperately to look away, afraid for our eyes to meet

Staying away for years trying to keep my feelings hidden inside
So afraid to let you know you send my heart on a roller coaster ride

Looking into your eyes, seeing just what's inside your soul
Longing and awaiting the day when in my arms, you I will hold

The first smile, the first kiss, the first encounter, I just can never forget
Waiting for the moment when seeing day break doesn't make me upset

You and I, soul mates from the start
Afraid to let go, trying to protect my heart

Somehow you got inside and you have captured my soul
Your words simply have me under control

Your every touch simply makes my body shake
At the moment of climax it feels like an earthquake

I've never known love like this before, the feelings cannot be explained
Love so good it makes me forget my own name

Separated by many miles yet feeling like your right next door
Memories are embedded in my mind, and within my heart forever stored

I'll never love another the way I love you
This love is so uniquely genuine that I'll never be able to love two

All I can say is, no matter what we go through
My heart will always belong to you.

DO YOU REMEMBER?

Do you remember the very first time we kissed?
I am so mesmerized at how impossible it is to forget

I remember the passion, I remember the wait
I remember it all including the date

Your lips were so soft and your tongue was so warm
I wanted so badly to hold you forever in my arms

I never imagined I could feel this way
Wanting and desiring to kiss you everyday

Your kiss was like candy, one just wasn't enough
Holding back the passion I feel is really getting tough

I hate that I have to share you
But because I love you so much, I do what I have to do

We've shared so much and we've been through some rough times
But I do realize now, no better friend will I find

One that will love me through the good and the bad
One that will hold me tight when I'm feeling sad

Waiting for that special day when you will surely see
That I love you far more than you will ever be able to perceive.

NOBODY LOVES YOU BETTER THAN ME

No one will ever love you better than me
My love is genuine it comes to you unconditionally

I love you when you're happy and even more when you're sad
I love you when you're being good and even when you're being bad

I love you when you shut down and want to be left alone
I love you even when you refuse to answer your phone

I love you whether you're slim or you've gained a pound or two
I love you because your size doesn't matter, you are still you

I love you when your hair is down or pinned up in a bun
It seems like the more I love you the further away you run

I love you to much to hurt you, and too deep to make you cry
I seem to love you stronger when we don't see eye to eye

I'll love you if you're dirty; I'll love you better when you're clean
I even love you when you're just being mean

So now you see, can't anybody love you better than me?
And all I ask in return for my love, is your honesty!

WILL WE EVER PART

Sleepless nights, I toss and I turn
Thoughts of you and your touch I yearn

Why does love have to hurt so bad?
Why do I find myself simply feeling sad?

I can't help but love you I've tried to let go
But I can only fool my mind because my heart truly knows

That the love I feel for you can't be buried with lies
It only covers it for a moment, then suddenly, the real emotions begin to rise

I can't eat, I can't even sleep
Thinking about you and wondering about me

Am I crazy? Have I lost my mind?
Laying awake at night doing nothing but crying

I just can't explain it; you tell me what should I do?
I can't help myself; my heart is in love with you.

I keep telling myself that it will never be
Yet I find such fulfillment even in the memories

Thoughts of those kisses we've shared so tenderly
I know you haven't forgotten, you remember every time you see me

What can I say; you fill a void in my heart
And no distance, time, or space will ever keep us apart

"Why can't you see you are the world to me?"

So Glad You're Mine

You cook, you clean, and you even do the laundry too
I sometimes sit and wonder what my life would be like without you
Imagining waking up and not finding you here by my side
The thought of your not being here one day brings tears to my eyes
So often we take one another for granted forgetting to show we care
Thinking in our hearts that the other will always be there
God has blessed our union from the very first moment we met
In the midst of everyday living, expressing our appreciation
for one another we sometimes forget
You have taken very good care of me and the children
and I know it hasn't been easy for you at all
Sometimes your body is so tired I'm afraid you're heading for a fall
You've done so much for me that saying thank you just doesn't seem to be enough
Watching you and not being able to help out is really, really tough
I believe in my heart that God has a blessing waiting just for you
Because of the sacrifices you make, and the loving things you do
I know I don't tell you often enough but you are truly one of a kind
You do what most men wouldn't, and I'm so glad that your mine

The Love of You

Its 4 o'clock in the morning and sweet thoughts of you invade my mind
Realizing that a love like ours is so very had to find
A love that is patient and longsuffering too
I feel extremely blessed because God sent me you
To have and to hold until deaths do we part
I'll never forget the day you truly captured my heart
Many ups and downs, problems that once seemed to be so huge
Thinking back on them now, realizing that they were quite minute
We've seen some hard times not always believing things would turn out alright
Often times wondering if the love we shared would sustain us through the fight
Realizing now that true love will enable you to endure heartaches and pain
Surprised to discover how love will bring sunshine in the midst of all the rain
Situations were sometimes so bad that I felt like we wouldn't last another day
With one look deep into your eyes I knew I couldn't throw it all away
We both have our differences and our disagreements too
But there's one thing I know, I have the love of you!

Longing For You

You went away and it was as if I could no longer breathe
Realizing that you were no longer here, was hard for me to believe

When on the telephone, the sweet whisper of your voice resounded
Fighting to hold back the tears, laughter is how I responded

Awaiting that great day when you would return
Laying awake at night crying while I yearn

Praying daily for my lover to return, to hold me, to
touch me, make me feel alive again
See he's not just my husband; he's also my best friend

When I'm hurting he's there, when I'm lonely he's by my side
Now that he's away, my insecurity I can't seem to hide

Never realizing just how much you truly mean to me, I
can't begin to imagine you forever staying away
The minutes turn to hours, the hours soon turn to days

The days grow longer, and I realize that my love for you is true
Each day I grow weaker, continually longing for you

Passion

Passion burning deep down inside,
Uncontrollable urges getting too strong for me to hide

Longing for that day, when our souls will be bound as one
No longer fantasizing, the battle will have been won

No one there to tell us it's wrong
Only the love we feel in our hearts beating strong

As we lay resting in each other's warm embrace,
Looking deeply in each other's eyes as the tears run down our face

Tears of pleasure, not tears of pain
Realizing that we have a unique love that no two others can claim

I long for you, your smile, and every inch of your being
Longing and awaiting that day when there will be no more disagreeing

Abandoning the fears, and embracing the truth
Realizing that the passion we share is only you for me and me for you.

I'm a Jewel

This can't be happening, someone tell me it's not true
They say that the one I love is madly in love with you
What does she have that's better than mine?
Is it that long black hair or that flimsy behind?
Or is it that she'll ride and I love to drive
Well shoot me for being confident, well balanced and full of pride
Don't get me wrong I love you, yes I really do
The problem is that you don't realize I also love myself too
Too much to continue to be a fool for you
Now here's the ultimatum, this is what you must do
Pack your bags, and keep on moving on
I no longer need your validation because I'm proud and strong
I sure hope it was worth it, you got what you wanted, and lost what you had
Don't you think for a moment I'm going to sit and continue to be sad
Since you're happy I won't dare stand in your way
You'll look back and realize that you lost a uniquely designed jewel one day

Time to Move On

Cried so many nights, can't seem to find any more words to say
Searching for a real love, yet looking for it the wrong way
Realizing that real love is not something that can easily fade away
Yet once you betray love, it's almost impossible to make it stay
Being hurt by the one you love is not something you ever forget
Trying to put your life back together again not knowing what to expect
So many questions, and never an honest reply
Yet you continue to stay, convincing yourself to give it one more try
Trying to keep the faith while praying for the hurt to hurt no more
Wanting desperately in your heart to walk away, walk right out the door
Looking back over your life wondering what all the sacrifices were worth
Remembering the constant turmoil and trying to erase the hurt
Love is an emotion, a small word with a very large meaning
So many times we mistaken love by comparing it to a good feeling
Real love has no limitations, no excuses, and no conditions
Real love makes no wrong choices or unexplainable decisions
So what good is a love when all the trust is gone?
That's no longer a love, so you might as well move on

I Can't Help Myself

I don't know why I love you like I do
Especially when I've come to realize that I'm not supposed to
You belong to someone else and I just get to borrow you sometimes
The only problem is that, we so often run out of time
I've tried so hard to erase you from my mind, to diminish the memories in my head
Never again to hurt, remembering that your not mine but theirs instead
But every time I close my eyes it's your face that I see
Suspended in time, baring your soul to me
Telling me just how much you truly do care
Not fearing that it's wrong, just being determined to stay here
Why are you embedded into every section of my heart?
Why can't you fade away and I just make a brand new start?
I want so badly to touch you, kiss you, to feel your warm embrace
Yet every time I think about it I am reminded of my place
In my place I have to let go, free you from my mind,
and try to think about something else
But how can I free you from my heart? I just love you and I can't help myself

Love Won't Go Away

Just need to talk, no need for you to reply
A listening ear is all I need while I wipe the tears from my eyes
Maybe you can understand the emptiness I feel deep down inside
Seems like there's no happiness no matter how hard I try
Somehow I thought that out of sight meant out of mind
But now I realize it doesn't work, when a soul mate you can only once in life find
I told him good-bye and I knew it was the end
Yet 600 miles away I still long for his touch again
Yes it was wrong but the love is still real,
unconditional, agape and longsuffering too,
Memories keep me smiling on the outside yet crying on the inside and feeling blew
A love like none I've ever known before and I fear I'll never know again
Yet everyday seems like I've moved on, only to start with a new reminder of my sin
A sin that I can't seem to find forgiveness for
Maybe because in my heart I long for him the more
I've prayed, I've cried, trying to erase what I feel in my soul
Yet every thought and every dream, his face I can still behold
I don't understand why it just don't all go away
Is it that I will love him forever and a day
How do I move on? How do I obtain a peace of mind?
Tell me the truth, true fulfillment and happiness will I ever find?
Not expecting an answer just needed to talk to someone who would understand
Just how hard it is to love and long for that one special man

Make Me Whole Again

Late night hours, I sit with thoughts of you on my mind
Trying so desperately everyday a little bit of peace to find
Tears fill my eyes when I remember all the wonderful times we've shared
The soft touches you gave that let me know you truly cared
The laughter, the joy, the sadness seems all so real now
Never imagined it would bother me, not having you around
Lord I just don't understand the longing within my heart
Why didn't it fade away when we decided to part?
Could it be love? Is that why it hurts so bad?
This is not how it's supposed to be, am I supposed to forever remain sad
Lord I don't understand, you said you wouldn't put more on us than we can bare
Can't you see my heart is breaking, is it that you no longer care?
Lord please help me, fill this longing that torments my soul
Fill this emptiness so I will again feel whole

Sent By God

I asked the Lord to send someone special to me
Someone who would accept me for who I am, and not what they wanted me to be
At first I wasn't sure if you were the one
Then when we expressed ourselves I said, let his will be done
The Lord will lead us and if it's meant to be
We will be together from now until eternity
I care for you in a special way and the reason is plain
We are both growing together in Jesus name
If it's his will we will be married someday
And we will raise our children in the same holy way

You're Always There

When everything in my life seems to be going wrong
You are right there trying to help me be strong
When no one else wants to try and understand
You're the one that's always willing to hold my hand
When things get so bad that all I can do is cry
You are there to wipe the tears from my eyes
When all my hope is gone and no one seems to care
Just the sound of your voice let's me know your there
So whenever there comes a time when I feel I can't hold out
I will remember your love for me and try to overlook my doubt
I'll hold my head up high and remember within my heart
That you're the one who loves me although we're miles apart

Our Blessed Love

The love we share is special, it was sent from up above
I prayed for someone with whom I could share my love

At first I didn't want to let my feelings show
I was afraid to love and I didn't want you to know

So as time went on the Lord blessed us
Now we share our fears and we've learned how to trust

No one really knows what you mean to me
Soon we'll be married and start a family

I know within my heart our love was blessed
The Lord will guide us and we'll continue to live in happiness

Just For Being You

You are the light that shines in that place far away
You are what make life happy day to day
Whenever there is a pain, that wound you always heal
That's why the love that you express one can always feel
So never change your loving ways because of what others may do
Remember I love you, just for being you!

The Love We Share

Having you in my life has brought me so much joy
The thought of you someday not being here I try to ignore
We've been through some rough times but that's all a part of life
We've always managed to work on the problem and everything turns out alright
You could never know how deep my love for you flows
Words can't begin to express the feelings for within the heart they grow
The passion of our union when lying in each others arms
Makes me feel secure, protected from harm
Love is such a beautiful thing when it flows from heart to heart
Although sometimes things get hard, real love will never part

MARRIAGE

M - Is for the many changes we will have to make
A - Is for the aggravation that can never turn to hate
R - Is for the reassurance of knowing your love is there
R - Is for the reality of knowing that you care
I - Is for the irresistible emotions that I have inside
A -Is for the anger you sometimes try to hide
G - Is for the glow that shines in your eyes
E - Is for the everlasting years of compromise

Put it all together and you are sure to find, that marriage takes work and time

The Meaning of Love

Love is an emotion that is sometimes misunderstood
Love is sometimes lost trying to decide if it's bad or good
Love is not something that can be weighed or measured
Love is a gift from God that must be treasured
Sometimes love slips away by an unshared feeling or an unspoken word
Love should be made known, not stagnant by a sword
True love is a feeling that never dies
It is so joyous that it doesn't want to hide
Don't allow love to be overthrown by tradition
Make your love known by pledging your devotion

I Never Thought

I never thought there would ever be
A perfect man made especially for me

But how can it be that you are mine?
Is this just some trick of time?

I've always dreamed of having someone who'd believe as I do
Someone who would accept me, and baby, along came you

See, you have renewed in me a light that was somehow hidden
I guess all I really needed was a new beginning

I've never had anyone who loved and cared for me as much as you do
And that's the type of assurance I'll give in return to you

I've prayed so long for someone like you, and God has answered my prayers
I pray that you will forever be by my side and our love will always be here

Just let us never forget who our creator is
Remembering he makes everything begin and he can also make them end

"I am yours, you are mine, we are God's, let's keep it that way"

Impeccable Wishes

So many times I sit and wonder if you'll ever really be mine
I guess all it really takes is a matter of time

I've tried so hard to circumvent my true feelings for you but I never seem to succeed
Could it be that I should belong to you, and you should belong to me?

I remember sitting by the window wishing for someone like you to come along
And finally when you did arrive I thought that our love was wrong

I've waited so long for this moment to come and now I don't know how to react
With such a beautiful proposal as yours, how can I hold back?

Now that we are together as one I am no longer sad or blue
I realize that my impeccable wish has finally come true.

A Reward Is Waiting

A marriage will never be all that you would like
Sometimes you may have to cry all night
Sometimes wondering to yourself if you can make it through,
Many situations arise and you don't know what to do
Then you stop and think about the love you feel inside
Saying softly to yourself, I'm glad he's by my side
When confusion comes and you can't seem to get along
These are the times when you may have to give up the right for the wrong
Though it hurts in the beginning you can smile and say
I know I will receive my reward someday

DA-JA-VU

There you are, like a ray of sunshine
I've seen this moment before, in the corners of my mind

Your beautiful face, your touch, your kiss, your sincere embrace
Visions of your body in my mind as we lay face to face

No distracting thoughts to invade our moment, just the reality at hand
Nothing to stop us from doing what only you and I can understand

Feelings flowing, going far beyond what our imaginations could perceive
So overwhelmed from anticipation, we simply forget to breathe

Here we go, it's really happening this time
I can feel the warmth of your touch as your lips meet mine

Your smell, your touché, your taste is the driving factor in my heart
This takes me to a place that I can't easily depart

I've seen this moment before, can it all be true?
Maybe it's just another moment of Da-Ja-Vu.

True Love

True love comes once in a while; they say we'll know when it's true
Sometimes when love comes we smile, other times we feel sort of blew
We never know whether love will last or whether it will fade away
We just take a chance on it in each and every way
When true love comes it fills our heart with joy everyday
There are times when we feel afraid and send love on its way
But if that love was meant to be the chance is worth taking
And if that love is not meant to be, then the heart is worth breaking
So when true love comes we will know it deep within our hearts
Then for the two of us life will have a brand new start'

Can't Live Without You

Sometimes I sit and wonder how life without you would be
Full of pain and heartache and tears flowing freely
Just to think of this terrible life brings tears to my eyes
Knowing that without you I could not survive
No distance in this world could take my love from you
So no man, woman, or human mortal would try to
I love you so much that words couldn't begin to express
But the good Lord up above knows what is best
One day will come when one of us will be gone
But I'll always have your love even if I find a new home

Fantasies

Sometimes I sit around and fantasize about you
I think of how our love could be so honest, so lasting and true
And I know that we would make it to the top
"As long as we are in love the fun will never stop
I thought of how much fun it would be running through the park late at night
And how sharing our differences when we were alone would be so right
I know this is only a fantasy and it may never come true
But we could make it a reality as long as you continue
to love me the way that I love you

I'm Lost without You

When you left I thought it would be easy
Now I see it's not as simple as I thought it would be
The love we once shared cannot be erased
Each morning when I awake I miss seeing your smiling face,
Before you left we both said things we didn't mean,
Forgetting the love we have, we both spoke nasty and unclean
But now I realize that love and time heals all wounds
I've had a chance to realize that I really do need you
Let us try forgetting the past and starting anew
Because my love, I'm lost without you!

Let Love Be Your Strength

No one understands the pain you feel but Jesus and thee
The joys, the laughter, and the everlasting memories
It seems as though sometimes the cross gets too hard to bare
But remember Jesus is still there beside you, your load he's willing to share
But in every life there's a milestone that must be tread
The best thing during a storm is knowing the other one is there
Draw from each other's strength; know that your love will see you through
No obstacle is too big as long as there's the two of you
Cling close to one another let every moment be filled with love
Lean not to you own understanding, let the peace come from up above

We Should Be Free

When we first met I felt things I've never felt before
Even through my pain, with you, I was able to find joy
We wanted so badly to be together day and night
We began sleeping with each other knowing it wasn't right
Our love grew so quickly that I began to become afraid
Wondering if you would always be there, or someday go away
There was nothing that you wouldn't do to try and make me happy
I felt as though you deserved someone better than me
When we got married we shared the same mind
Then after a while, joy we could no longer find
You were determined to do things your own way
Never stopping to consider if I had something to say
You began to treat me like a piece of luggage you owned
And I was supposed to follow you, disregarding that you were wrong
After praying so hard I felt like it was all in vain
Then my heart began to fill once again with pain
I can no longer take the things you're putting me through
I've tried so hard, but now there's nothing more I can do
I thought that we could make it, maybe I expected too much
I believed that our love would be strong enough
But now even the love has somehow began to fade
That's why I feel it's time for me to go my way
I want you to know that I really tried to be a wife to you
But you didn't want a wife, you wanted to rule
It's all over now, and my heart is filled with sadness
But I believe, this is for the best
I wish things could have been different but I see they can't be
That's why I've decided that we should be free

My Dying Love

You have hurt me and my heart is torn apart
I thought that we were off to a brand new start
When the baby died I blamed myself
I felt all alone as if nothing was left
Then you would come and show me your smile
That's when I believed I could hold on for awhile
I thought that you loved me; I know that I loved you
But it has to go both ways, not just me loving you
I thought I had one thing in this world to call my own
Now I see that all my thoughts were wrong
Your love I can no longer feel, and the pain is so deep inside
At this moment, I still love you, but I'm afraid someday soon it will die

Loneliness

My heart has been broken, one too many times
I poured my heart out to you, all you told me were lies
You said that you loved me and I believed that your words were true
I realized that you didn't love me, as much as I loved you
Sometimes when I would go out, and come in sort of late
I thought I would find you sleeping and discover that you were awake
And now that our love affair is over, and my fling for you is gone
I realize that my expectations of you were a bit too strong
So as we go our separate ways let's go knowing this is what's best
Let the memories that we've shared take the place of our loneliness

Tears of Life

The tears of life have fallen from the eyes of my lonely heart
And as they roll beneath my chin, the pains begin to start
I've tried so hard to cease this worry in my head
But it only seems to deepen, and this I really dread
Many nights in my bed I cry very silently
Saying softly to myself is this how it's supposed to be?
I've always dreamed of love and how it would make you happy
But I realize now that my dream was only a fantasy
Why all the misery? Why all the pain?
Why can't love be simple and not have to be explained?
Love will never be that easy, but I hope one day to see,
A time when man and woman will share in love eternally
Without woman having to worry about any rivals that come her way
Because she will know that he is hers forever and a day
But until this day comes my pain shall linger on
Awaiting that wonderful day when my heart can sing a new song

Confusion

Here I am thinking about you after having set you free
Wondering why things couldn't have been better between you and me
I've always dreamed of us getting married and raising a family of our own
But I can't dream of this anymore since now you're gone
I've tried so hard to deal with you; I thought my love would be enough
But I soon realized that things were getting a little too rough
Sometimes when you love someone, they're all that matters to you
Regardless of the wrongs they do, you feel that love will bring you through
Then when things don't work out, the light in your life becomes the dark
Somehow deep down inside that love's fire still holds a little spark

My Hurting Heart

Somehow, Someway, Someday we will make things right
In our hearts we'll be as one, and not just in our minds
I've given to you even when I've needed
Overlooking how badly I had been treated
When I'm gone I guess then you will see
I stayed simply because I believed you were a part of me
I've hurt, and late at night I've cried
While you lay there sleeping without a care in mind
I've shared, and only God knows how much I've cared
But you never knew, because your heart was never there
Someday I know we'll make it through
Someway, I know you'll see as I do
I pressed on, I pressed over my pain
Just to try and make my life worth living again
I know with joy there comes some pain
I know in every life, we see a little rain
But when does the sun shine through?
When will there ever be a me and you?
Whatever is going to be, just let it be
Even if it means setting you free
Maybe this is all there is,
Maybe I've given all I have to give
Time to let go, let's begin a separate start
Disregard these tears that's falling because of my hurting heart

We're No Longer Together

Time has gone by so quickly, it seems like only yesterday
We were walking down the isle, my dad was giving me away
Things have changed so much since we've been together
At first I thought that our marriage would last forever
But now I see I was wrong, and deep down inside I feel bad
Wondering to myself if this is what God had planned
I've tried so hard, only God knows how hard I've tried
Sometimes pressing over a broken heart and tear filled eyes
Only he could help me to pull myself up and to go on
Realizing that in the end he will restore my joy
But now I've come to the end of my fight, and the war has been won
Not realizing I was the winner before I had begun
I had so many dreams, so many desires too
Now the dreams are gone, I don't know what to do
Always being knocked down and taken advantage of
Then all you ever say is, you know what I feel for you is love
How can you love someone when you don't allow them to be themselves?
Instead you try to change them and make them someone else
I walked around with a smile but inside my heart was crying
Not wanting anyone to know that my love for you was dying
I can no longer hide it, I've hurt enough
If I have to hurt, I'd rather hurt by myself
We're no longer together and maybe it's for the best
Somewhere, someone else may be waiting for you and can stand the test

I'll never forget the laughter,
I'll never forget the tears,
I'll never forget the pain in my heart,
That I carried around for all these years

Good-Bye My Love

Love is an emotion that is sometimes misunderstood
Though it brings you joy, it's not always good
We sometimes love so much that it hurts us inside
And because we were so trusting that pain we try to hide
We allow ourselves to be touched both physically and mentally
Hoping that right by our side, that lover would always be
Once the love starts fading we get worried and confused
Trying hard to figure out, what was it that I didn't do?
Saying what have I done to deserve such pain?
I've given all I have to give, taking nothing for my gain
Love doesn't always know just how real to be
Afraid of being hurt, yet not wanting to remain free
Love always needs someone to help it work and grow
If love was not an emotion would we know which way to go?
A life without love would be empty and cold
Having no one to hug, touch, or hold
Love sometimes works in strange and crazy ways
But the joyful moment it brings, is worth the cloudy days
I'm glad I've learned to love though it hurts sometimes
If it wasn't for the rainy days, I couldn't enjoy the sunshine
What I've shared with you is more precious than pearls
Time has taught me that were living in two separate worlds
I guess it's true, all good things soon come to an end
I hope that we can part and still remain friends

Take care my darling; I will always love you in my heart

Object of My Desire

When I lay down at night your there beside me
When I awake in the morning, your lovely face is the first one I see
When all around me seems to be going wrong
I find comfort by lying in your loving arms
You are my friend, my partner, my love
Looking deeply into your eyes I realize that you're a blessing from above
Sometimes I'm afraid that our love is not enough
Sometimes, I wonder why times get so tough
Whenever I feel lonely I find security in your embrace
Knowing you are a product of God's amazing grace
I'm so blessed, to have you in my life
Many times I lay awake reminiscing at night
When we share our differences the ecstasy goes untold
Only the moment of exhaust shows how deeply our love unfolds
You're the object of my desire, can't you see
There will never be another for me

The Game Must End

I don't know how much more I can take
I do not know how much longer I can wait
Waiting for you to trust in me
Waiting for you to allow me to be free
Free in the spirit to sore like the birds
Returning to the nest where their first chirps were heard
Why doest thou continue to persecute my soul?
Is my very being too much for you to behold?
Why not, just set my soul free?
Why be a hinder to you and me?
Time will never heal the scars from the past
How much longer do you think this game will last?
If the trust has been lost as we both know it has
Why keep pretending that this too will pass?
Let's not continue to make fools of ourselves
Let's let this go, maybe one day there will be someone else
Someone who can be all you want them to be
Right now I can see it's obviously not me
We'll never share the same dream
I can only be who I am, and maybe that seems mean
But why change me, when you refuse to change yourself
Why try to change the hand that has already been dealt?

Good-Bye

What do you do when everything is going wrong?
Who do you run to when you feel that love is gone?
What do you do when the hurt is so deep that the tears will not flow?
How do you continue to smile so no one else knows?
How many times can the heart be broken before it no longer mends?
How many names can you call me and still call me your friend?
Too much pain, too many tears
Too much sacrifice, and too many years
No more crying, no more hurt
No more praying for this love to work
In time maybe the wounds will heal, maybe they will only fester
But for my health I believe that separation is better
Done all I can do, I refuse to do anymore
So now I say good-bye as I walk out the door

All That's Left of Me

All I have to offer you right now is a woman with a broken heart
I can't promise you diamonds or pearls, all I can promise is a brand new start
No I'm not perfect, born with flaws like everyone else
All I can do is work at loving you while trying to perfect myself
I am damaged goods you see, a misfit is what I am called
After going through so many trials trying desperately not to fall
But everyone has their breaking, point, and I guess that I've come to mine
Never expecting to fall at this point and time
Counting it all joy now realizing I've fallen in such able hands
Strong and yet firm, the makings of a real man
Knowing that true love is the core of our existence
Not having to worry about being disrespected as a form of consequence
I come with mixed baggage, some of which only your love can set me free
And all that I can do is give you all that's left of me

Right Love at the Wrong Time

The pains of life are falling from the eyes of a broken heart
Remembering where the joys began and where the sorrows start
How can a true love cause so much pain?
A love that carried so much value only to have been found in vain
How can something that felt so right turn out to be so wrong?
How can something that felt so good cause so much harm?
The hardest part of it all is having to say good-bye
Never to see your face again or hear your voice echoing in the sky
Better to have loved and lost than never to have loved at all
Visions of what we once shared will remain a distant memory in my heart
So now I say farewell to my once lover, my friend
Though it seemed as if it was the beginning we now know it's the end
Although the pain we now share is real, I know we will both be fine
We had the right love just at the wrong time

Unchained Memories

You came into my life like the breeze on a hot summer day
And like the leaves on a palm tree my heart began to sway

Beating to the sounds of what now was a different tune
No longer playing or moving to the songs of gloom

The whisper of your voice was like rain falling from the skies
Eventually covering the tears running from my lonely eyes

You bring me joy unspeakable with just a thought of you
And the feel of your caress so firm and yet so smooth

As we go on living day to day
Remembering every moment of our last embrace

Like a caged animal I have now been set free
Only by your love and our unchained memories

Why Trust?

Trust is a fragile emotion that somehow remains strong
Trust quickly fades away whenever it has been wronged

Once trust is lost it can take a lifetime to find again
Especially when it's lost by a spouse, a loved one or a friend

Trust is easily offended by jealousy, silence or deceit
Trying to regain trust is a fight that's hard to beat

Only a willing heart can overcome the hurt and pain
But if it's not a team effort, things will just remain the same

If you truly love someone and the trust has gone away
Maybe the only thing to do is to go your separate ways

Knowing that true love can overpower any pain
If your love was real you'll find each other again

To live without trust can never be a happy life
Each and everyday will be filled with misery and strife

So why go on when your emotions cannot be true
Only you can control what's inside of you

If you decide to continue together make sure you forget the past
Because if you don't the relationship will never last

Cries in the Night

Often I find myself weeping for no apparent reason
It matters not what time it is, nor what season
Sometimes I wake up in the middle of the night and find dried up tears on my face
And I also find that I have tossed and turned all over the place
I find myself feeling bad and always looking sad
Even after I have received the best experience I ever had
But these feelings always seem to come over me,
When my soul is happy or my mind is free
Even when I'm not worried I have the urge to cry
But someone always comes along so I hold back the tears from my eyes
I know that I'll find happiness if I keep searching far and wide
Then when that right someone comes along, my feelings I'll no long have to hide

I'm So Very Sorry

I know I've hurt you, but it was not intentionally
I want you to know just how much you mean to me
Your love is more precious than silver or gold
That's why I need you here in my arms to hold
What I've done, I never meant to do
Regardless of my wrongs, my heart belongs to you
I've cried so many nights knowing I've hurt you
Just give me another chance to prove my love is true
Only God knows how much I care for you
Since you've been gone I don't know what to do
I know that we can make it if we give it one more try
Just give me a chance to wipe the tears from your eyes
Right now my heart is filled with pain and worry
Hoping that you'll believe me when I say, I'm so very sorry!

We've Only Just Begun

As we stand and make our vows, we make a brand new start
I can feel the love we share flowing from heart to heart

I've been waiting for a long time for someone like you
Someone that I could give all my love and devotion to

My love for you keeps growing strong
That's why I know it can't be wrong

Troubles may come our way and we may sometimes disagree
But I will always remember, I believe in you and me

Whatever comes our way were going to make it through
No matter what other may say or do

Today marks the day when we become as one
And yes my love we have only just begun

No Matter How Far

Distance could never take away the love that you and I share
The lonely hours that pass by in my thoughts I know that you care

With each passing day I long to be in your arms
Then I began to think of how you're feeling with me being gone

No man in this world could ever take your place
My body trembles all over with just one thought of your handsome face

Just keep in mind the love that I have inside for you
And you too will begin to feel as I do

To hear you say you love me gives me a reason for living
And no distance could ever stop our love because it's never-ending

Without You.........

Sometimes I am afraid that you might go away leaving me with only
your memory, never to see your face or hear your voice again

Sometimes I am afraid that someday will never come, that you will be taken
away and my dreams will die. And I will only live wanting to touch you

Sometimes I am afraid that my star will fade away into the sky and never to
return and that's when I look up to see it shine, darkness will be my only vision

This Roller Coaster Ride

I've never had a friend quite like you
So many mixed emotions inside that I don't know what to do
I'm afraid of what I'm feeling, afraid of what the outcome will be
Afraid of destroying something that means so much to me
But it's hard to ignore the passion I'm feeling deep down inside
Often times laughing when those feelings begin to rise
Can I ever be able to satisfy the needs you have inside?
This is just one of the questions that haunt me at night
With every new question, arises a new fear
Wondering constantly after each kiss where do we go from here?
Is it wise to move forward, is it safe to give in to what I feel?
Or is it best to ignore it and pretend that it's not real?
We'll never be able to openly express the passion that's felt within our hearts
People would never understand how something like this could ever start
We carry ourselves with such high standards, both desiring the very best
Demanding to have things our way refusing to settle for less
So how can we be secret lovers and yet remain best friends?
How can we continue to be together and never give in?
Wanting so badly to touch you silky skin
To hold you gently in my arms, to kiss you again and again
But this is only a fantasy one that I hold dear
Never being able to reveal it but knowing that it's real
So I'll just hold on for now keeping it all inside
I find joy in knowing I'm not alone on this roller coaster ride

How Can We Go On?

The love is so very strong but the pain keeps getting greater
I keep telling myself things will get better, but as I
look around the hour is getting later

To Late to ignore the feelings, to soon to tell the truth
To painful to hold on, yet to afraid to turn loose

I've given this love all I have not holding back anything
Yet in all reality she's wearing your diamond wedding ring

The passion is so rewarding and the pleasure is so very real
But now it's time to let go, time for us both to heal

Sleepless nights are getting tiring; eating is not even a major part of my life
All because the man I'm in love with, my soul mate, comes along with a wife

How can we go on with so many limitations?
There are so many hopeless dreams and so many pointless expectations

I've put my whole life on pause just to start our life on play
When really I don't feel like you're in my life to stay

You were here for a season and now that season has changed
The sunny days we've shared are now filled with rain

Too many mixed emotions, to many confused days
To much to endure and still give God the praise

To heavy a load to carry a burden that's not my own
You belong to another, you have another home

So where do we go from here? I really need to know
Let's just turn and walk away, let's just let it go

Held Memories

Lips so soft and gentle, pleasing to the skin
Wanting so desperately to taste them again and again
Realizing with ever kiss I'm desiring more and more
To one day fulfill this fantasy that I so often endure
Exploring your beautiful body inch by inch not looking at the time
Just knowing that at some moment our bodies will intertwine
That will be the moment when there will be no where to run
Reality will be here, my fantasy will be done
You will get that moment to express what you're feeling inside
Exploring your every thought, no longer having to hide
Allowing yourself to feel and be felt in return
Not having to worry, long or yearn
Maybe all this is just my great imagination
Maybe it will never happen but remain an expectation
How can this be happening, these feelings that I have inside
Wanting everyday to have you here by my side
Waiting each day to hear your sweet voice
Wanting each day to see you sometimes having to accept your choice
Realizing that you have something that I could never give
But believing deep within my heart, with my love alone you can live
Knowing that it's real and it's coming from my heart
Not having to wonder if or when we'll have to part
The feeling that went through me when our tongues met
Immediately my body responded and I began to sweat
One never knows what each new day will allow us to see
But I will always hold that wonderful moment in my memory

That Special Part of Me

When I first saw you, it was truly love at first sight
The gleam of your smile was so bright, I hated to say good-night
Your touch was so tender and yet so true
My every thought was filled with visions of you
Instantly I knew that one day we would be as one
Shortly there after our shared lives had begun
Like sand in an hour glass that continues to flow
With each new day our love continues to grow
Lying together in each others arms, I soar into ecstasy
Believing that when we awake I'll find you next to me
Just to see your smile fills my heart with joy
Knowing that we will be together forever more
Your soft sensual kisses send chills up my spine
From head to toe, time after time
You are my partner, my lover, my friend
You are that special part of me that ends and begins again

The Love of My Life

When I first saw you, I couldn't believe my eyes
I was looking at an angel with no disguise
Soon after we met we became a pair
Hugging and touching knowing each other was there
Now I realize that we're not just a pair we are one
Yes my dear, after twelve years it seems we've just begun
You're more precious than diamonds and worth far more than gold
I feel my heart skip a beat every time your hand I hold
When I awake from sleeping your beautiful face is the first I see
When the sun goes down at night and the moon rises,
in my arms is where I know you'll be
As I watch you sleeping with your skin glistening like the stars
I think to myself, how lovely you are
The warmth of your body is like the delicate petals of a rose
I can't begin to explain how your touch makes me explode
You are my wife, my joy, the love of my life
The air I breath, the song my heart sings, my everything

Crazy Love

What am I to do with the feelings I'm trying to hide?
How do I manage to keep it all inside?

Never imagined that this would come to be
Me loving you and you loving me

How am I supposed to turn loose, how do I let go?
Knowing how I feel inside yet trying desperately not to let it show

I wish I could walk away, act like none of this exists
But in my heart I know this will always remain a wish

You've touched a place in me that I never knew was there
Sharing my emotions and feelings when it seemed like no one cared

You came along at a time when my life held a great void
Your love was able to fill me, in my heart it is now stored

I've spent several nights crying wanting to set you free
Only to realize that you have become a part of me

It seems as though no one can hurt me as easily as you can
And still through the hurt I will extend to you my hand

When I don't hear from you it's as if I'm incomplete
Only to go home at night and not be able to sleep

As I close my eyes I see your face smiling back at me
I can even remember watching the tears as they rolled down your cheeks

Wanting so desperately to take all the pain away
Realizing that I could make it all better with one simple embrace

Then I awaken to touch the reality at hand
This crazy love that I feel for you I will never understand

When you're All Alone

Why do I continue to love you when you have hurt me so bad?
Why do I continue to care when the very thought of you makes me mad?
What kind of love would take this hurt over and over again?
What kind of love would make me still call you my friend?
Why do I stay? Is it something wrong with me?
Why do I continue to cry endlessly?
Don't you see the hurt? The pain you're putting me through?
Maybe you just don't love me the way that I love you
You take my love for granted, but one day it will be gone
Then you will realize the jewel you had when you're left all alone.

How Do I Let Go

When we first met I was intrigued by you
Your kind and gentle ways told me that you had feelings for me too
As time went on I tried to stay away and keep my feelings inside
Realizing that you belonged to someone else and so did I
Finally it happened, I found myself sheltered in your arms
Not realizing at first that I was causing any harm
Not only to myself but to all those involved
Now where at a point where the problem must be resolved
I must let go, I don't know how, but I do know why
Although it brings me great physical and mental pleasure it's not right
I don't mean to hurt you, believe me I'm hurting just as deep
But I have to turn things loose; I have to set you free
Let's go back to before the passion, let's go back to being friends
Let's release the past and begin again
Yes it will be hard to forget all the shared times
But we know that this is the only way to be at peace in our minds
My love for you will never change, my fear is that it will only continue to grow
If our love is real, God will bless it to remain and grant it to someday be so

What Do I Do?

So many tears, can't cry anymore
So tired of searching for love and only finding a closed door

Wanting so badly to find someone who understands
Someone who can feel my pain, someone willing to hold my hand

Knowing in my heart that only what's done for Christ will last
Praying and hoping that someday soon this pain will pass

The pain in my heart, confusion in my mind
What can I do when no peace can I find

Wanting so badly to do what's right
Yet longing inside, finding it hard to fight

I know that loving you is wrong
I tell myself to flee from you, stand and be strong

But I can't hide what I'm feeling inside
So many mixed emotions, how do I decide?

I've come to a crossroad and I know I must choose
Do I go with principles or Love? What do I do?

JUST KEEPING IT REAL

No more lies, no more deception
No more acting like there's no form of affection

I love you and I know you love me too
So why do we keep lying the way that we do?

Who is it that we are trying to convince?
Why do we choose to lie to one another then take offense?

Taking offense because we know how we truly feel
Afraid of what other's might say if they knew the real deal

Okay we'll just keep playing, acting like there's nothing we feel
I don't know about you but I love you, and I'm just keeping it real!

DON'T TAKE YOUR LOVE FROM ME

I love you, and I refuse to let you go
It doesn't matter to me if the whole world comes to know

May seem crazy but believe me it's true
What you need to understand is that there's no me without you

You are my soul mate, my one and only true love
I place no one before you besides my Father above

I know that there are obstacles that we must endure
But I'm willing to take that stand because I know our love is sure

Driven from the very depths of our souls
Anticipating that great day when I can have and hold

No longer having to leave and return to being bound
No longer being on an emotional roller coaster going round and round

Because of your love I believe I can conquer all
Because of your love I can stand and not fall

We have become one, and it's you that makes me complete
Take away all that I have, just please don't take your love from me

I JUST CAN'T STOP LOVING YOU

So many tears cried, just don't know what's going on
Loving you so much, yet knowing that it's wrong

Trying so hard to erase the memories from my mind
Realizing that there not just my memories alone, there yours and mine

How can I let go, how do I forget about you
How can I erase a love that makes me feel brand new?

Maybe it's all just my imagination, and you really don't love me
Even if it's not real, it's real in my heart you see

Your always in my thoughts, It's your face I see when I close my eyes
It's the longing I have to hear your voice, that often makes me cry

Just the sound of your voice makes me feel complete
Thinking about you sometimes I can't eat or sleep

How is it possible for me to feel this way?
Why can't I just close my eyes and all the feelings just fade?

Because what I feel is real, not acceptable that's true
But I can't help who I love, can you?

I've tried to ignore my feelings but I don't know what else to do
I just can't stop loving you.

I Sought Thee, and Found Thee

I sought far and wide, for someone who'd be true
And when I'd finally given up hope, into my life walked you

I thought, because of our differences the love would not last
Later the differences slowly began to pass

The days went on, and my eyes held a certain gleam
Our love began to grow stronger as we shared each other's dreams

It seemed you were an angel, sent especially for me
I'd finally found someone with whom my soul felt free

What only seemed to be a dream, will finally be done
Two separate hearts beating will now beat as one

I sought thee and found thee, now I'll never let you go
And were taking our vows to secure our love and letting everyone know

"WHAT GOD HAS LOVINGLY UNITED, LET NO MAN SEVER"

Imagination

Midnight has come, and I can't sleep
Visions of you invade my mind making my body weak

So much turmoil inside my mind
Wanting you, needing you, no substitute can I find

You're the one and only, no one could take your place
As I lay here and try to sleep, I close my eyes and I see only your face

Staring back at me with that big beautiful smile
And as I reach out to you, I pause for awhile

Realizing that your not really here, it's just my imagination again
I open my eyes with a smile, only to turn over and imagine all over again

Say Your Name

What I wouldn't do to spend one night with you,
Holding you, touching you, tasting you too
Warm juices flowing from your body to mine
Both of us elated, suspended in time
No limitations, only ecstasy and exploration
Climax so intense it surpasses our wildest imagination
Here we go, come on, let's take this ride together
Slowly, faster and faster as our bodies begin to quiver
Wow, there it is, can you feel what I feel?
Up on a mountain, now sliding down a steep hill,
Joy unspeakable, too powerful to explain
All I can do now is say your name

Me and You

I hear you speaking, but can this be true?
You want me, just as much as I want you!

Is this real, or is this some kind of game?
All this time, pretending that you didn't feel the same!

I was so afraid that my passion would turn you away
Trying to hold back emotions, watching what I say

Only to hear you now say, "I need you"
Although it brings great joy to know, it brings along sorrow too

Realizing that I'm miles away, there isn't much I can do
Only hope that you will hold on to that passion until I return to you

Counting down the days, the hours, the minutes, the seconds, I must go through
Until I see the day when you appear, and we're one, no longer two

So let's keep it real, let's be honest and true
When the time is right it will only be me and you

There's No Limit

How I long to see your face,
to feel your touch, your warm embrace
To have you near all through the night,
Hugging, touching, squeezing you tight
Showering you with compassionate love,
A connection so tight, it fits like a glove
Slowly stroking your body from head to toe,
Moans so quiet no one will ever know
The passion, that burns as the love juices flow,
Louder and louder we become as we go
Deeper and deeper into our own wonderful world,
One to one as we twirl
When we'll stop, no one knows,
For there is no limit to how deep love goes

Deep Inside

Minutes turn to hours, hours turn to days, days turn
to months, and months turn to years
Years filled with longing and tears

Tears from missing you and wanting to have you near
To talk to, to cry with, to lend a listening ear

Passion burning inside heating up till I'm flushed in the face
Holding, kissing, touching me in just the right place

Relaxing as the juices flow, from me to you and from you to me
Exhaustion settling in as our souls becomes free

Anticipating so long for this very day,
There's no turning back now, were on our way

Soaring toward a new galaxy called "love beyond measure"
Feeling each other deep inside is a gift to be treasured

Do you love me?

How much do you love me, that's the question in my head
Do you love me enough to tell me the truth, or will you tell me lies instead?

Afraid that I won't understand or that I might walk away
True love covers a multitude of sin, and grows stronger everyday

Yes we will get angry and no doubt upset at times
But a real love finds a common ground and makes peace inside the mind

As you know, making up is often the very best part
Even in the midst of the pain, and the hurt that's in the heart

I just don't want to cry anymore, I'm tired of going there
Tired of hoping to have you to myself, only to find out I have to share

What do I have to do, how much more do I have to give?
Before you realize that it's for your love that I live

I've tried so hard to believe that your love for me is true,
Knowing that there are other's what am I supposed to do?

I'm too far away to keep the worry in my head
I guess you'll know my real love for you, once I am dead!

I don't know what else I can do, how else to let you know
They say if love is real, you'll know by letting it go

Well I did, and here we are together again
I guess this means our love was meant to last until the end

Tell me you love me, and convince me that it's true
There is only one love, that's me and you!

Love Hurts

We started out as friends and who would have knew
That one day I would fall head over hills in love with you

Neither of us could have imagined that our feelings for each other would grow
Taking us places in our minds that no one else would ever know

To afraid to talk about our feelings, to afraid to let them show
Yet loving each other so much, unable to let love go

Suddenly in walks another, what am I supposed to do
Expecting in my heart that it would someday be just me and you

Trying everyday to make you happy, waiting patiently to have you to myself
Only to discover that you're in love with someone else

All this time loving, trusting, believing in you
Only to discover, you were playing me for a fool

So disappointed, my heart ripped apart, I feel the pain as it bleeds
Realizing that the one I love never really loved me

Never imagined you would ever be like everyone else,
Taking all the love I have to give then leaving me by myself

I've been hurt so much; I believed with all my heart
that you would be the one to understand
Just how painful it would be to fall in love and be hurt again

How can you say you love someone and take no regard to how they feel?
Maybe it's me who needs to just keep it real

Bandage up my heart; realize that it just didn't work
Love doesn't love anyone, Love just hurts

Family

Mother

Sitting here doing nothing being work free
I began to think back on an old memory
I began to think about the times that you held me tight
Whenever I would have a bad dream and wake up crying during the night
I all too often think about the way you washed away my tears
By telling me it's alright and loving me through my fears
There were times when you should have punished me, but you let me slide
I never would question you but I'd go to my room and wonder why
I appreciate your kindness and everything you do
Of all the mothers in this world, there will never be one as great as you

I love you Mom

A Mothers Love

A mother's love is a special love, one that can't be brought or sold
It's a feeling that stays with you whether you're young or old
Whenever I'm feeling lonely and it seems as if no one cares
I just call on my dear mother for she is always there
Remembering in that day, mothers love was all we had
When daddy died everything seemed so lonely and sad
She tried with all her might to bring us up the right way
Sometimes we felt that she was too hard, but I thank God for her sternness today
Mother your love has taught me so many things in life
It has taught me the difference between wrong and right
When I was taken away and locked up thinking I'd never be set free
You were the one there taking care of my children for me
When I got burned out, trouble and fear didn't want to cease
Seeing your face mother, gave me such a feeling of relief
Knowing that while you were there everything would be alright
I could close my eyes and sleep peacefully at night
Words cannot compare to the love that you've given me
And kind deeds could never repay you, for I've learned a mother's love is free

Only You Dear Mother

You were there when I was hurting, lonely and in despair
No one wanted to be bothered, but you mother, always cared

When I felt like giving up, letting go of the faith
You mother were always there trying to keep my pathways straight

Whenever I was in trouble or I had done wrong
You were there mother, standing stern and being strong

It doesn't matter now what people might try to say
You were always there mother in each and every way

Though I never knew how to express my gratitude for all that you would do
This one thing remember dear mother, I loved you

Even in my final hour you were there to hold my hand
Somehow I knew you would be, because you always tried to understand

And for the love you've given me through the years,
memories of you follow me in measure
For in my life dear mother you were my most valued treasure

Mother's are A Lot like Jesus

She will try to protect you and shelter you from harm
She will continue to love you in spite of what you've done wrong

She will try to instill in you the righteous way to live
Always reminding you that it is more blessed to give

Mothers sit awaiting, and heeding their child's call
No matter how many times that child may stumble or fall

Mothers are sometimes tough so that a lesson you will learn
Sometimes she has to let go so that your own way you can earn

Mothers have days of suffering and nights that seem very dim
But if the load becomes too heavy, she knows to call on him

Like the eagle that protects her nest, she feels no fear
She too will sacrifice her life for the child she loves so dear

Mothers are a lot like Jesus, look closely you can see
Nothing is more important to a mother besides God and her family

Daddy's Little Girl

Growing up as a little girl you long for a hero to call your own
So hard to find one when your father is gone
Yes Mother is there doing the best she can
There are just some things girls need to learn from a man
Like how to stand strong and what guys are just bad news
What clothes are too revealing and what lines guys will try to use
Somehow we search for that stern hand to hold us up when we fall
We look for that someone on whom we can always call
A father not just a man that was there for a little while
A father, a man that helps you go through the trials
A shoulder to lean on, someone to wipe the tears away
Someone who will be there in spite of your mistakes
Only time can heal the wounds of absence embedded in your heart
Everyday is filled with a new chance to fill an empty part
Someone to love you no matter what you go through
A father's love is a strength felt in the heart that's shared between us two

The New Arrival

The nights are slowly rolling around and the days are drawing near
I can't help but explode with excitement knowing that the baby will soon be here
Everyone keeps asking me what do you want a girl or a boy?
It really doesn't matter to me as long as it's healthy, that would bring me joy
I imagine watching my child grow as the days and months go by
Remembering all the sleepless nights because of the fearful cries
I think as I hold it in my arms, could this really be true?
I have brought something into this world as beautiful as you
Then I visualize that sad day when my child will no longer be with me
It would have gone out into the world to create its own family

The Miracle of Three

One, two, three gifts given to me
Never knowing how a gift could make your life complete
One was born a sure miracle in itself
Fighting battles with the enemy while trying to remain in good health
Then came number two, a sheer joy to behold
Eyes shined like diamonds, a smile worth more than gold
Finally along came an angel as lovely as can be
I just could not believe she really belonged to me
As I sat back and observed the work at hand
Realizing to myself that this was all in God's plan
He sat down one day with visions of me in mind
Drew out a road map along with some mountains that I would have to climb
Overcoming many obstacles yet holding on to faith
I found myself standing in a holy place
A place where God has total and complete control
As I travel day to day my hand the father holds
Three miracles he performed right before my eyes
Three children entrusted to me, the trinity is what they signify
All representing a three fold ministry, a battle that has already begun
Elijah the spiritual father, Ahmad the submissive son, and
Nhylah the prophetess, united they are all one!

My Little Angel

My little angel just as cute as she can be
Watching you grow everyday reminding myself of me
I see the beautiful butterfly that has left the cocoon
Watching you as you flap your wings under the glare of the moon
I can't help but get teary eyed when reality starts to sink in
My little angel is a little lady, her smiles glowing in the wind
How do I let go? She's my baby girl
How do I set her free in this cruel and hateful world?
I know the day will come when she will be grown
and desire to be free
But I don't care what anyone says she will always be a little angel to me

Sympathy

We Shall Meet Again

I am gone away now, there's no need to cry
I'm occupying my mansion far beyond the sky

No more worry, no more pain
No more sadness, nothing but gain

Beautiful blue skies filled with God's amazing grace
Listening to the angel's singing, finally beholding my Father's face

More beautiful than any could ever imagine it to be
Everyday dancing for I have finally been set free

My soul is now resting safely in his arms
No longer being concerned about hurt or harm

But don't be sad for me, my battle has been won
I am more than a conqueror, for I have overcome

Living life eternally is the reward I have gained
Rejoicing daily in my Father's name

So don't cry for me, rejoice as I do
Continue to run the race that my father has prepared for you

Believing by faith, that together we will be
Smiling, holding hands, walking in victory

So smile on loved ones, know that I am yet here
Remember that my love for you will always remain near

Just hold on to the memories, release all the pain
Press toward the mark, for one day we shall meet again

"In loving memory of Uncle Charles Stewart"

It's Gone Away Now

God gave me a gift, one I had longed for
No one could have known all the joy I had in store
Inside my heart I planned to decorate just for him/her
Fill a room with beautiful colors, fresh air and lots of love
Then something happened and my new gift was gone
All I could say was "what did I do wrong"?
I had no answers lying in that cold hospital bed
Filling as if my whole life was gone and I was dead
As I laid there under anesthesia all I could do was dream
Of how I waited for so long and now I don't have anything
But it's gone away now and I don't know how I'm going to stay strong
I pray that one day I'll be able to let go of this pain and move on

"Dedicated to my unborn child"

By and By

Things sometimes happen and we don't always understand
All we can do is trust in God and put matters in his hand
Believing that he is able to work things out alright
Knowing God works miracles in the power of his might
When all hope is gone hold on to what you feel inside your heart
Remembering that God had a plan right from the very start
Though the load may seem heavy and almost impossible to bare
Just look up and see Jesus for he is always there
When you feel like no one cares and you think you're all alone
Just call on Jesus, he will be your friend when everyone else is gone
Children are a very precious gift that comes from God above
Sometimes God sees fit to take them back, to shower them with his love
And although it leaves us hurting very deeply inside
Just know that they are resting peacefully, far beyond the sky
Just waiting for that special reunion when you'll see your child up there
When God comes back for all his children in the middle of the air
Whenever you feel like crying, go ahead and cry
Soon God will wipe away the tears, and you'll understand it better by and by

"In loving memory of Bryanna"

His Will

Oh my Lord, could this really be
The love of my life being taken away from me
Laying there in that hospital bed starring off into space
I can't help but wonder if he even remembers my face
This sickness came on so quickly that I haven't had time to think
I just sit here beside you and watch you as you sleep
Praying the entire night that in the morning you'll still be here
Not wanting to let you go, desiring to hold you near
Sitting here wondering, is there an unspoken word that needs to be said
Are there things undone, messages that have gone unread
Suddenly I stop and remember that God knows best
I must hold on to my faith and let my mind rest
Trusting that the Lord knows what's best for me
For it is his will that must be done throughout eternity

Remember Me

The time has come for me to depart
But don't you cry, don't be heavy in heart
I have done my job, my course is now complete
I have not been defeated I have not been beat
But don't cry for me just hold on to my smiles
Know that I am now resting, free from all the trials
No more heartaches and no more pain
No more sadness and no more shame
Just remember the laughter and all the good times we've shared
Remember in your heart that I have always cared
Know that I have been lifted no more burdens, I'm free
Don't remember the hurt you feel today, just remember me

Having a Bad Dream

Someone awaken me, hurry I'm filled with fear
Can this be real the love of my life is no longer here

Gone away, never to return again
What am I supposed to do without my best friend?

Go ahead they say, shed a tear, it's alright to cry
How am I supposed to cry when I'm so angry inside?

I'm left here all alone, doesn't anyone understand!
A part of me has died, this I cannot comprehend

No one to talk to, no one to yell, fuss or fight
No one there to rub my feet, and no snoring to keep me up at night

This is not happening, it's all just too extreme
Someone please tell me I'm just having a bad dream!

As Time Goes By

Things may be rough right now and no doubt very hard
Just believe within your heart you can make it with God
When everything gets quiet and all is completely still
Don't get downhearted just remember it was God's will
In the late night hours when tears fill your lonely eyes
Remember the good times you shared and watch the tears subside
See life is a challenge, and sometimes we have to cry
But things will surely get better as time goes by

Special

A Poem Just For You

Time could never take away the joys that we have shared
Though there were some bad times, I knew you weren't going anywhere
Whenever there was a family need you were always there
Showing us your love and letting us know you cared
Our love for you will never die and that you know is true
Because there were times when without you, we wouldn't know what to do
I realize that it's your birthday and I don't have much to give
But one day I will be able to express how I really feel
So this poem I have written just for you along with a birthday kiss
And hopes that this birthday will bring to you, your every wish

"Happy Birthday Sis"

Nothing to Give

Christmas time is here again and things are not the same
My Christmas this year is filled with heartache and pain
But there is one fact that always hold true
No one could ask for more than loved ones like you
Whenever I fall your there to hold my hand
When I feel like I can't make it, you let me know that I can
It hurts me so much inside to always have to look to you
But you're always there to help in spite of the things I do
This year I have nothing to give except the love that's inside my heart
And my love for you is something that no one could tear apart
Someday I know that things are going to change
Then I'll be able to give to you just the same
But until things get better I will make do with what I have
Although I have nothing, I still somehow manage to laugh
My caring is yours; my love for you is free
Someday I'll be able to give to you like you've always given to me

Merry Christmas

Special Part of Me

K - *Is for the kindness he always showed me*
E - *Is for his never ending energy*
N - *Is for the naughty things he helped us do*
I - *Is for the incredible dances that only he knew*
T - *Is for his tolerating me all summer long*
H - *Is for the hugs he gave me when it was time for me to go home*

Put it all together and it's plain to see, KENITH *will always be a special part of me*

What You Mean To Me

G - Is for the Godliness that you possess
L - Is for the love that you let manifest
A - Is for always lending a helping hand
D - Is for dedicating your time to understand
Y - Is for the years of wisdom you have gained
S - Is for your sternness when we need to be restrained

M - Is for the many trials you've come through
C - Is for caring when no one else seemed too
N - Is for never giving up the fight
E - Is for enduring our calls in the middle of the night
I - Is for the innumerable times you've helped us through
L - Is for the light of God that's shining inside of you

Happy Birthday

All You Are To Me

L - Is for the love of God that you possess
O - Is for your optimism when situations are a mess
R - Is for the reverence you display towards God
E - Is for how you try to eradicate the enemy with the word
T - Is for the tolerance you express towards me
T - Is for the terse conversations you give to set the captive free
A - Is for the way you admonish all to accept the love of God

Put it all together and your sure to discover a very important part of my life, YOU!

Never Shall Forget

Never shall forget the times you prayed for me
Never shall forget the times you prayed that I might be set free
Never shall forget the tears you shed for me at night
Never shall forget how you encouraged me to fight
Never shall forget how you wondered if I'd ever learn to stand
Never shall forget how you said to hold on to God's unchanging hand
Never shall forget the many scoldings along the way
Never shall forget the hugs you gave that made me stay
Never shall forget the day I spent with you
Never shall forget you washed my feet and I washed yours too
Never shall forget the days you shared in my joy
Never shall forget you're telling me that Jesus was not a toy!
Never shall forget the day you endured unthinkable pain
Never shall forget how you stood strong in Jesus name
Never shall forget the strength of Sampson that you displayed
Never shall forget how you're still standing strong today
Never shall forget the many prayers you prayed on the phone
Never shall forget you taught me that I'm never alone
Never shall forget that there's someone along with
momma that's always praying for me
Never shall forget that it's my spiritual mother "Alma Jean"

You're My Strength

When I'm gone don't weep for me
For I will see you again, this I guarantee
There may be miles between us but were near in our hearts
What seems like the ending, is only a brand new start
It's too hard to say good-bye so I'll just say so long
Knowing that if God gives us grace someday I will return home
You will always be in my heart no matter where I may be
See you don't understand you have become a very important part of me
I love the Lord and a lot of that love has been renewed by you
Don't worry Lucille, you've worked too hard for me to loose
So don't be afraid, I'm determined not to go to hell
I know sometimes by my actions you can't really tell
But believe me, I'm sincere when I say
Because I love you so much Lucille, I will see you in heaven one day

A SPECIAL BIRTHDAY MESSAGE

This message comes late, but it's more special than the rest
Because it's filled with a love that can be felt when expressed

You're another year older, yet your beauty remains the same
Because it comes from within it will never change

To express it simply is truly hard to do
Because your not simple, you're an extra special you

Material things I have given but they someday will fade away
So this time I'm giving of myself so it will stay with you day after day

Your physical beauty goes far beyond measure
Your inner strength is truly one to be treasured

You're caring touch, and your generous thoughts
Are remembered with every beat of my heart

Your worth far more than rubies and your more precious than gold
Your love is so special is should be bottled up and sold

But that would only prove just how special you truly are
Because a love as precious as yours couldn't be put in just any old jar

It would have to be lined with gold and wrapped with purple you see
Because in my eyes you truly are royalty
So I send this special birthday message, in hopes that you will see
You not just special on your birthday, your special everyday to me

"Happy Belated Birthday Moose"

www.ingramcontent.com/pod-product-compliance
Ingram Content Group UK Ltd.
Pitfield, Milton Keynes, MK11 3LW, UK
UKHW020141250726
13967UKWH00002B/793

9 781425 119812